MINDFULNESS FOR DANCERS

Corinne Haas

For Those Who Love To Dance.

"*There is a vitality, a life force,
an energy, a quickening, that is
translated through you into action,
and because there is only one of you
in all time, this expression is unique.
And, if you block it, it will never exist
through any other medium
and will be lost.*"

— MARTHA GRAHAM

TABLE OF CONTENTS ✐

INTRODUCTION

When I was a little girl of three, my mom did what many moms do: she signed me up for dance classes. For budding ballerinas at this age, of course, classes consisted of children running around the room jumping over pretend rivers with scarves, using chopsticks to count the rhythm of whatever classical piece was playing on the record player, and relishing in the joy of movement.

This was my first introduction to the ballet world.

I loved to dance and yet I truly despised putting on the pink tights and black leotard that were the uniform of our local studio. It felt excruciating to be forced to conform and adhere to such strict discipline at a young age. So as would be true of my pathway throughout my dance career, I quit early, only to return a couple years later. At age five I began my lifelong complicated relationship with dance.

From the time I was a child until well into my teen years, and I am sure many of you can relate, my local dance studio became my second home, one in which I would spend countless hours. The two men who ran the studio became my surrogate parents, guiding me through a world to which I only had access through their training. Their commitment to the world of dance was a gift and inspiration to me and many others who continued on into professional careers.

To say that I loved dance at that time in my life would be an understatement. I loved it, like many of you, with all my heart and soul. It wasn't just the pure joy of movement, but also the act of sheer willpower and the challenge of the discipline. The power behind the technical side of ballet is what drove me. I could find my inner strength in the dance world through my focus and determination, which wasn't always the case in the "real" world outside of dance. The dance studio provided a stable environment and daily place in which I could immerse myself and grow.

My heart came alive with the rituals of being a dancer: the studio, the stretching, and the first plie. All of it was my gift to me. There was pure satisfaction in walking into the studio alone and discovering new ways to open myself up and be challenged. The empty studio was a

new frontier that was a rote routine only on the surface. Underneath that surface was the opportunity to tap into a flow or rhythm unfamiliar to every day "normal" life.

As I grew and developed into my teens, my passion for dance didn't lessen, but the number of other interests, pressures, and demands increased. I was trying to balance new friends, school, pressure from my parents, my dedication to dance, and the possibility that dance might not lie in my future. My body also changed and became more rounded and curved. I had breasts and hips, which in truth I didn't mind, but which were not a good fit for the dance world. And right there with that seed of self-disapproval, held within the tender time frame of adolescence, my internal struggles with body image and weight began. I mean, how do you honor your body and despise it for being something it is not? My early teens were an incredibly confusing time period, particularly as boys began entering the picture. I felt as if I were running two parallel lives and neither one satisfied a deeper truth within me.

My life shifted again around age sixteen. Following a summer intensive, I was accepted for the year-long program at the San Francisco Ballet. This was amazing! To be around other dancers who shared my intensity and drive to perfect our craft, to be together with a shared passion, to join a professional company—I was all in! I can still feel the excitement and pride I felt at being asked to train in such a professional atmosphere. It meant an incredible amount to my self-esteem and confidence. The invitation confirmed that I was good enough to have dance become my lifelong career. A renewed dedication and confidence took hold that aligned me clearly on my future path.

I made many new ballet friends when our year began, and we were thoroughly immersed in the ballet world. We talked about ballet incessantly, stretched constantly, and ate meagerly. All of us were there because we were good at something, and this something was to be our focus and our commitment. We were a tribe of fellow travelers on the same journey. We were a crew.

But, as everyone knows, ballet is a competitive world, so although we were all fellow travelers, we were also competitors out to get a spot in a company in which there were few spots. I was lucky that the group I was bound with was quite fabulous. We managed to keep our competitiveness to ourselves and our friendship at the forefront—most of the time.

Life as a dancer in this environment was invigorating and yet quite stressful. I didn't realize until many, many years later how deeply uncompetitive I am. I immerse myself in a challenge or anything I am passionate about, but I don't feel driven to achieve something at the expense of others. During that year-long program, my heart struggled to find balance between loving something so dearly and competing against individuals whom I held just as dear. Dance and studio life ceased to be my safe place or home, and instead became an avenue for my future career. Perhaps I was too young for this type of pressure or commitment, or perhaps I was just the wrong type of person. As I have matured, I have learned that one of my deepest fears is of commitment. At that time, I could honestly only commit to myself as a dancer, a mover, a person whose purest desire was to perfect a craft that I held very deeply in my heart. I wasn't prepared to plan the rest of my life at sixteen.

Again, my weight became an issue. Looking back, I likely used weight to protect myself from committing to a singular career path that I told myself I wanted but feared. I think somewhere deep down I knew I wouldn't be able to maintain the skinny body or the level of discipline it would take to continue on this path. But as is typical of anyone who is in the midst of walking through a difficult ordeal, I couldn't see or hear my truest thoughts. And I didn't want to, because that might mean moving into unknown territory. So rather than deal with the emotions and fears that were just beneath the surface, I focused on my weight.

I was given all sorts of advice from my teachers: eat oatmeal each morning to keep you full throughout the day, eat the same thing daily for months to help your body process the food more efficiently. These could have been great pieces of advice, but considering they were coming from a rail thin teacher who chain smoked, I have a feeling her idea of what kind and how much food I should be eating differed from my own. I tried eating what a few of my fellow dancers ate to lose weight—rice at all meals, popcorn, bagel rounds with the inside part taken out, the list goes on and on. I am laughing right now at how crazy all of these ideas were and are. Our techniques were not effective or sustainable ways to lose weight. They were a quick-fix to a larger problem that was blocking me from getting what I wanted and what all of my teachers wanted for me. Looking back, I wish there had been a pause button, so that I could have looked more deeply inward to assess what I truly did want.

With all the different information flying around me during that phase of my life, I really wasn't sure who or what to listen to. My own internal voice was confused. I could barely hear it and perhaps, I didn't know what it even sounded like at such a young age. Because of this lack of clarity around who I was, I made decisions that I may not have made had I known some techniques to help me slow down my spinning thoughts about the future, press the pause button on my emotions, and just reflect for a moment. I wish that instead of telling me to eat oatmeal, my teachers had helped me understand that there was time to figure out the future. But these words never came. Perhaps nobody knew how to say it. And so I left the dance world again. To say that I regret leaving ballet at this time would be accurate. I don't hold many regrets in my life, as I see them rather as opportunities for growth and learning, but this particular moment still makes me think what if?

What if I had danced for one or two years with the company, realizing my fullest potential as a classical dancer? Would that have brought me closure and left me fulfilled? I will never know and that's okay because I most likely wouldn't be sitting here writing a book about mindfulness tools and techniques for you had I fulfilled my dreams many years ago.

There is a bit more to my story; it didn't end at sixteen. Though I did leave and return to dance many times from that point forward, three to be exact, I did find a new dance home when I joined Alonzo King LINES. I will always be grateful that I finally found a style of movement that was more in alignment with my natural body that was the perfect blending of classical and contemporary all in one. Alonzo also offered an incredible spirituality, not only with his choreography, but

also through his expectations for his dancers. It was rigorous, but also a supreme re-navigation of who I believed myself to be as a dancer. LINES opened my mind to new ways to move that were not confined to the classical structure.

I danced for LINES two separate times. Both were uniquely different experiences, as the second time around I had been "off" dancing for five years. I had to re-train completely to get myself back in shape simply to re-audition. I was elated when I was offered the position, as I was amongst so many other beautiful dancers who wanted the opening equally as much. But this was only the beginning of a new mountain I would climb; I needed to build my strength and stamina up to get back onto pointe.

As I reflect back, this period taught me an incredible amount about pure focus. I still see it as a time of sheer courage. I couldn't and wouldn't allow anything to get in the way of what I wanted to achieve. I had to let any self-doubt that crept in be dismissed from my thoughts, because it wasn't going to serve my highest potential or goal. Because of this deliberate dedication to my intention and goals, I learned some things about myself and life that I am passing along now to you.

A NEW LANGUAGE, A NEW WAY OF SEEING

This book offers a new way to see yourself. In it I offer a brand new perspective, drawing from both ancient and modern wisdom that I hope will give you some tools to work with on your road to becoming a professional dancer.

Since leaving the professional dance world twelve years ago, I have become a dance teacher and an intuitive life coach. As an energy worker and intuitive, I see my clients more as pure beings of light and less in terms of what they do for a living. They come to me because they are stuck in some way and need help re-gaining their sense of internal balance. I work at a soul level, which means I can see things that go well beyond the surface. It is a

gift and an absolute joy to be able to witness individuals in this way. This kind of witnessing—seeing someone in their purest energetic light—is a way of seeing that I believe has a place in the dance world.

As dancers, you are continually witnessing others' energy without even knowing this is what you are seeing. We often watch our peers or a performance and are unsure of why our eye is drawn to one dancer over another, especially when they are of the same high level of technical ability. All we know is that we can't take our eyes off whatever that specific dancer is exuding through their movements. We are caught up in their light and in their energetic vibration. This is such a common occurrence in the dance world that we don't often use the words to describe it as energy or light. We use words like artistry or expression.

In this book, I am asking you to be curious about yourself in a different way. I invite you to see yourself as a larger version of you—an individual with a vibrancy that is waiting to burst through all of the self-criticism and internal judgement you most likely listen to on a daily basis. I want you to begin to understand that you have choice as to what internal dialogue you listen to and recognize that it is okay to feel good about yourself. You don't need to operate from a space of depletion and self-doubt.

I learned an immense amount from the dancers I taught this past year about how they view themselves and the pressures they face daily as they strive to be better dancers. I found it quite sad at times to hear the level of heaviness and fear in their voices and thoughts, and the amount of pressure they all feel. Despite being some of the most beautiful, internally graceful and sensitive individuals one could meet, they never feel as if they have achieved much of anything. Dancers are special in so many ways and most of the time they don't even know it. One of the most common characteristics of dancers is their high attunement to an inner voice of perfectionism. I suppose that is what may make someone a high achiever. But we don't need to focus solely on the negative aspects of ourselves in order to get better at something. In fact, listening to our inner perfectionist most often has a debilitating effect on our artistic expression. The alignment is with the mind instead of the heart.

Through this book, I hope to take you on a journey to get in touch with your inner voice. I offer techniques and tools to support you in hearing that voice more clearly. Getting to know YOU in a bolder way takes courage—not only courage to push through into unknown territory, but also courage to sit in those times of doubt and the unknown spaces that exist within us. This territory can be scary. But it is the place that we avoid that has all of the answers we need to transform from one cycle into the next.

The visual of the caterpillar turning into the beautiful butterfly is a timeless metaphor for transformation. The caterpillar does not know or experience itself as anything other than what it is. But at a certain point, after eating so many leaves, the caterpillar is no longer comfortable staying in its current reality. It must, therefore, take time and space and go into a place of isolation, the cocoon, so that it may transform into the wondrous creature it was meant to become.

This process appears so simple on the surface. And we are always longing to transform into something "other" than what we are. But in truth, when we enter into the transformational process, when we go into the void or the darkness, we find that the cocoon is a bit more uncomfortable and potentially fear inducing than we had imagined.

I honor that the dance world will most likely not be changing its focus-driven intensity any time soon. I also recognize that it is not my role to try and change individuals like you, those who are attracted to the discipline and perfectionism of life as a professional dancer. Rather, I hope this book will open your mind and heart to the internal power you have right at your fingertips—especially if you are grappling with self-doubt, low self-worth, or any of the other depleting mind sets that go hand-in-hand with the dance world. I hope this book will help you to come back into a place of balance within yourself.

HOW TO USE THIS BOOK

I have a fondness for serendipity. I wanted to create a book that was an easy go-to because I often feel the best insight comes when we are guided to something—a certain page or chapter—and find what we are looking for sitting right there. I rely heavily on my

intuitive guidance to get me through my day and my life. In fact, I wouldn't have a job if I didn't honor this aspect of myself in its fullest regard. I am often guided to open a book or take a look at a certain page to gain some information that I am searching for and not finding outwardly. This process triggers me to make a new connection point or to integrate new pieces of information to existing pieces and connect the dots. You know that moment when you are dancing and "everything" you have been working on up until this one point comes together? It feels like magic when that occurs, like a magical moment stopped in time. But in truth these moments can and do happen all of the time if we pause and take a moment to make space for them.

So enjoy your time with this book and think of it as a new kind of studio space, one in which you are invited to center and connect to your deeper wisdom. A simple, small moment of guided reflection can go a long way to supporting your transformation into a more grounded, artistic version of the person and dancer you are now.

SEEING YOURSELF AS ENERGY AND LIGHT

We all carry our own light internally. It is what makes us special and unique. We each have been given a light that sometimes shines more brightly than at other times. As dancers, we are linked to this light because it is what makes our artistry visible. We are vibrant because we are in our fullest expression of self. Our artistry is our internal light shared with the world through our artistic voice. In the world in which I work, this vibrancy of artistic voice begins as an energetic impulse, which can either shine or be blocked depending on many factors. This energy is like a beautiful stream or river that runs up and down your spinal column from the base of your spine to the top of your head. It is a river that is uniquely patterned after you. This is you in energetic form.

With this river of energy as your first point of creation in form, we want to begin using the language that is most resonant with the more intuitive side of your being. This vocabulary is based in visuals, vibrations, colors, and sensations, etc. It is based on emotion, cycles, seasons, the rhythms of life—all these things that we sense are around us at all times if we could pause and take a moment to make space for them to be received.

Our artistic voice flows through and with all of these currents of energy. They are tools that are simple and always right before our eyes. Problems arise when we continually strive, drive, and push toward achievement that is when this language and vocabulary gets muddled. So this book is an invitation to remember the softness and gentleness of self-care. Because self-care can move mountains. Self-care offers the freedom to surrender into the deeper part of you that has all of your intuitive language moving through you at all times.

Let's begin.

ROOT

MOVING FROM STRENGTH

When I was a young girl I couldn't keep my feet still. I was always moving or turning while my mom was talking to me. I am sure my mom found it an annoyance and most likely assumed it would stop as I got older, but thankfully, it never left me, because dance was my love.

As dancers we are blessed with the ability to defy gravity and fly through the air, to expand our range of movement in the most imperceptible of ways. To move becomes so commonplace that a fouetté or a grand jeté becomes part of your normal, and standing becomes foreign. When you stop to think about how remarkable that is, I hope a large wave of gratitude washes over you.

When we speak about moving from strength as a dancer, I know the first image that pops into my mind is of a dancer doing lots of sit-ups or strength training to help support and build their muscle stamina. And since our body is our tool it must be treated as a fine piece of machinery that we care and tend to on a daily basis through a healthy diet, rest, and pre- and post-dancing exercises. But I invite you to expand your range of understanding to experience the body from a deeper, more internal space—one that opens the body up to another level of awareness, an unseen avenue for health and recovery. The root of our being is at the base of our spinal column and can be referred to as the central "home" of our bodies. When we are moving from strength as we dance, we are asking that point of our body to be aligned with all of our grand movements and then help us "come home" at the end of a long day to a space of internal healing.

To be in our bodies while we dance is to hold a very fluid awareness of the earth as the springboard for all of our movements. Even when we stand at barre and begin our first pliés, we are grounding our low back, legs, and feet and asking them to grow roots directly through the floor. And when we are done with our day, we ask the same of our bodies: to bring the energy back in to a deeply rooted place in our body that will allow us to truly rest. The interchange of energy flow from our body to the earth and then back in to our body through our leg channels allows for a continuous and natural life force to heal and rejuvenate our tired legs.

GROUNDING

In the energy world, to ground means to ground your energy into the earth. To ground means to allow the earth to support, replenish, rejuvenate and restore your body to a natural place of balance. Our sense of feeling grounded or rooted within our own being arises when our internal energy feels balanced and in harmony within itself.

Envision that you have lost the cord that connects you to the center of the earth. That cord has somehow been cut or has unraveled to sheer threads and left you swaying in the wind. You have no home base and are running wildly from one thing to the next. You may feel scattered, as if you have figuratively left parts of yourself all over the place: at school, the ballet studio, with friends. The same discord can occur when we are in the studio. We are focused on so many different things: checking our technique, perfecting it, remembering choreography, wondering what our teacher or director is thinking. So many thoughts are running through our minds that we forget sometimes how to be centered in our own bodies.

Rest assured we all experience this disconnect at moments. It is natural to become unrooted when we get hit by too many internal and external pressures or have a schedule that doesn't leave much room for us to pause and ground ourselves, a necessity for professional dancers and artists. When we ground our bodies we release the day's tension and return to the earth's center for renewal. Just as drinking lots of water flushes the lactic acid build up out of our muscles, so too the grounding cord releases the energy and tension that have built up within our spinal column. Grounding results in one big energetic and physical wash.

EXERCISES

1. Envision a cord running into the center of the planet. In the evening, or at night before bed, sit on the ground or in a chair, and take a few deep breaths to relax the body from a long day of dancing. Place your attention on your very low back at the base of the spinal column and begin to grow a root into the center of the planet. Give yourself time to release the tension of the low back and spine down and out the root and back into the center of the planet.

2. Consider: During your dance breaks, did you chat with friends, look at your phone the whole time OR did you take a moment to sit, take a deep breath, and ground your body for five minutes?

3. Take time to be close to nature. Sit or lie on the ground to relax the body and connect with the earth. Remember its capacity for renewal and rejuvenation. Allow the earth to support you.

BEING IN PROCESS

In the dance world, the word process is used quite frequently to describe a desired approach to any choreographic piece we have been given. We are asked to be "in process" with our movements and the flow of the choreography. The word in and of itself is beautiful and one that I absolutely adore. I use it quite frequently with the work that I do, as I am either analyzing my own process with creative projects to better guide others with theirs, or I am helping my clients understand the nuances of the process they are walking through with their own projects.

To be in process means to be smack dab in the middle of whatever you are focusing on. It is not the beginning of a new project, a period marked by excitement and curiosity, nor is it the end, when the final, joyful push to completion occurs. When you are in process you are in the middle territory, and sometimes you may feel lost.

The word "process" itself offers no set framework to hold onto or any bullet points to follow. Instead, the simple, energetic value of the word suggests an explorative nature, a curiosity about the unchartered territory of our internal landscape. The lack of restrictions or structure may evoke fear in some. They may

see only chaos. In others, however, this process may serve as an invitation to challenge their own creativity to the fullest extent.

How you approach life and new challenges may determine how you perceive being in process. You may be someone who jumps in immediately, someone who holds back and waits until you know all of the information, or someone who falls somewhere in the middle. All are great. You were born with a certain disposition, and this disposition shapes your pathway and life. Knowing what category you may fall in will only serve to give you more information on your approach to new situations and learning new choreography, which will help you to be kinder and less reliant on comparing yourself to others. For instance, if you are someone who likes to take your time with learning something new, and needs more processing time, you may need to honor that by not immediately comparing yourself to someone who jumps in. Give yourself some space to be you, which in turn may free up energy for your learning to naturally come more quickly.

To be in process is to ride the wave of a cycle and a cycle is a framework of time that has a set beginning and endpoint. Sometimes the beginnings and endings of a cycle are obvious and at other times less so. Nonetheless, there is a beginning and an end, whether we know it or not. In dance, the concept of process is the same. In each of the works of choreography we are given there is a flow to the movements. It is up to us, as dancers, to find the natural pace and curvature the movements share with us. It is as if the steps can speak and we are bringing them to life through our own artistic translation.

Alongside the process of learning a new piece of choreography, there is also an emotional process that is equally important. In dance, we mentally run a dialogue that is quite perfectionistic. It can get the best of us, especially when we are in the process of learning something new. I remember beating myself up at every turn with a new piece of choreography. I would get mad at myself for not getting the choreography quickly enough. Then I would turn around and berate myself for not executing the choreography well. And if that wasn't enough, I would again turn on myself and get upset that I hadn't added enough of my own artistic expression into the new piece. Talk about stifling process. The dialogue I just mentioned is the exact opposite of being in flow with your own emotional process. We need to give ourselves permission to honor the frustration, anger and tears that come up during the middle period of any project and resist the voice that says we are too slow or that someone else could have done this much better. As artists, an openness to process and a willingness to move away from terms like pretty, ugly, bad and good will allow us to give full expression to our creative voice and spirit.

EXERCISES

1. Envision your emotions to be part of, not blocking, your artistic process. They are there to serve the fullest expression of your artistic voice, instead of hinder it. The shift in perspective that invites your inner world to support your process as an artist is a bold and courageous move in the development from dancer into artist.

2. While you were in dance class today or learning a new piece of choreography, did you begin to feel bad about yourself? Were you sad because you began comparing yourself to others? Turn your emotions into something positive. Take your emotions and shift them into a visual that you can use like a color, texture, or shape. By expressing your internal emotional dialogue through your movement in a constructive manner, you may find your artistic voice coming alive.

3. Begin writing in a journal and keeping track of what types of situations make you feel emotional and unable to stay present with your dancing. By tracking the cycles of your emotions you may be able to identify and work more effectively at using your process to its fullest to support your artistry.

CORE

MOVING FROM POWER

When I reflect on my younger self as a dancer, I don't remember too many moments when I felt very powerful. I remember feeling a lack of confidence despite my abilities as a dancer. In fact, the way I felt each day was truly based on how much attention I received from my instructors. I relied heavily on their validation to know how I should feel about myself for the rest of the day. If I received a lot of attention and critique I felt as if I had worth; if I didn't receive feedback, I felt that I wasn't doing something right. In some ways my response makes sense, as the entire structure of classical ballet encourages dancers to strive for nothing less than perfection. But when I really look at how much I relied on others' validation, I feel sad, because I lost my connection to my own personal place of power.

Moving from power, as I want to define it, means being empowered. To be empowered means to walk with a sense of self that no one can take away from us. It is not based on anything external. It comes from a deep, internal place that gives us the feeling of certainty in who we are and where we are heading.

The internal place of empowerment that I speak of resides right in the middle of our belly, just beneath the diaphragm and right above the belly button. When we place a hand here it feels like a nice mid-way point between our upper and lower body—a resting point to bring us back into center. The idea behind moving from power means that we use this energy point to reclaim our own internal sense of validation for all of the things we bring to our dancing. We renew and define our value daily.

When we wake up each morning, we don't always feel a strong sense of empowerment. It is quite natural and expected for our energy to fluctuate from day to day. I see a lot of different helpful advice on how to push through the dark days in magazines. I believe this is all empowering and wonderful, but also lacking a broader perspective, especially for dancers. Because dancers have the ability to push through anything and are quite good at overriding their own emotions and pain thresholds to do the art they love, they need a daily check-in point that allows them to get to know the truth of how much power they are walking with each day, so that they can make clearer choices with their bodies. In doing this, they get to know their own natural rhythms and internal power points, so they may become empowered to trust in themselves and navigate their day more efficiently.

AWAKENING WILL

Our will is in direct alignment with the core of our body. This central spot is our force, identity, and will power. We need this point to bring about focused action and ignite change within our lives. In the dance world, we need all of our will to execute our desired movements, but more importantly, to keep us on track with our desired goals.

When we begin the journey of awakening our internal will, we must first understand what it might look like from an energy perspective. One of my favorite visuals for this point is a fire in the belly that can burn brightly or softly depending on the day, and one to which we have a direct link, that helps sustain our energy and focus. The idea behind this fire is that it is always burning. It may be a small flame at times, but it never dies out.

We may ignite the power to achieve and change our lives through this point. It is the energy behind any goal we choose to go after. We need this energy, or fire, while dancing to create certainty and conviction with our movements. When we are struggling to successfully make a balance or turn, this point may give us a visual representation of the energy necessary to override depleting thoughts, make the physical adjustments, and regain our will. It is a great visual tool to add to any moment we are feeling a bit off physically and emotionally.

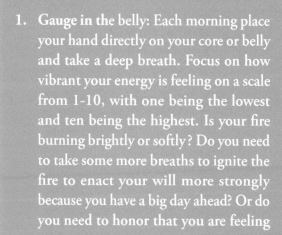

EXERCISES

1. **Gauge in the belly:** Each morning place your hand directly on your core or belly and take a deep breath. Focus on how vibrant your energy is feeling on a scale from 1-10, with one being the lowest and ten being the highest. Is your fire burning brightly or softly? Do you need to take some more breaths to ignite the fire to enact your will more strongly because you have a big day ahead? Or do you need to honor that you are feeling

less energetic today, and perhaps need to adjust your day, keeping socializing to a minimum and tuning in to use that energy for your movements?

2. Remind yourself daily that you have an internal core point that allows you to choose how you will approach anything you are given. Use this internal point in times of weakness or lack of confidence to know that you always have a strength that lives within you and is always there to guide you through your day. Place a hand there anytime you are feeling low self-esteem.

3. Change your life today by choosing to take one small baby step in the direction of a better you. You will be that much closer than if you choose to do nothing. Small steps add up to big changes in the end, so learn how to enact your own willpower and motivation and you may just surprise yourself at what you can create.

GOAL SETTING

Setting a goal is by far the most amazing gift we can give ourselves. It asks us to begin creating focused intent on something that we would like to see ourselves grow into

> ⟩CORE : *Moving From Power*
> **VIBRANCY COMES FROM WITHIN**

or become. Setting goals is a wonderful way to enact our willpower and get used to our personal reaction to pushing our boundaries.

For me, goal setting needs to have one important element: courage. First and foremost, goal setting entails the courage to dream of a more expansive version of you and also the courage to creatively set very small baby steps to get there. No step is too small. A nice visual I always like is the idea of lily pads or stepping stones on your way to your ultimate vision. This visual allows for a nice compartmentalization of all that I have to do. I have to say that sometimes, my first lily pad is just me sitting with the idea of what I am about to embark upon; I love this dreamy phase, and it aids me in getting a sense of how near or far

I am from my goal. It is important to have a glimpse of how much work you will need to be putting in, though once you embark on your journey, you may

find that you overestimated how close you were to your initial goal. I then begin to create my first initial action steps. And having worked with many different types of individuals, I can say that sometimes the simple act of even making a list is the first baby step since there is so much nervous excitement around the proposed creative idea. So you see, no step is too small to honor.

So face the fear and the uncomfortable anxiety around reaching for something beautiful for yourself. These are necessary and normal emotions, especially when you are pushing yourself into new terrain. If you didn't feel these emotions, I would be worried that you may have set up a goal that was too easy. So give it a try and see what visuals you can come up with to support you on your way to embodying your dreams.

EXERCISES

1. One of the best and most influential ways to accomplish your goals is by seeing them. Create a vision board specific to you – one that encompasses all that you are through imagery, color, favorite quotes and objects. Use anything that helps you to remember how special and important you are to this world. Make sure to place your board somewhere in plain sight, so that it can support you daily in remembering the unique and special qualities of you.

2. Design and create 3 action steps to begin achieving your goal. Do this to break up any feelings of being overwhelmed, which can occur when you have created a large vision for yourself. These baby steps will be just the right combination of will and action to take you closer to your goals.

3. Make a list of all you want to achieve in the near future and put it up on a piece of paper in clear sight. The paper needs to be the first thing you see in the morning and the last thing you see before you close your eyes at night. It is similar to a vision board but a more direct visual with bullet points or numbers.

HEART

MOVING FROM BALANCE

I remember those beautiful moments while dancing when everything was in alignment and effortless: the studio fades away and you feel like a fairy floating on the breeze. Your movements are executed with ease. Your technique carries you and allows you to give full expression to your artistry.

In one way, moving from balance is why we dance. We want to feel those physical moments of flight. In fact, we live for those simple bits of freedom with movement: when we strike a statuesque arabesque or hold a passé that could last for days, we feel completely in the moment and balanced.

Understood from an energy perspective, moving from balance means that we have an emotionally balanced heart center. We are not triggered by the ups and downs of life, but instead respond with generosity and kindness to others and, most importantly, ourselves. This center is our most vulnerable spot on our body and therefore a bit tricky to keep balanced. We get emotionally hurt quite easily and throw ourselves out of balance when we put up any type of emotional protection, which definitely doesn't serve our art form in any way.

As dancers our heart center is our most expressive place on our bodies. The small spot right between the two collarbones, in particular, is our avenue of artistic expression and voice. If this area is collapsed in any way or held too tightly based on limiting beliefs about ourselves, it shows. We can actually see that negative thinking block our heart space as the gateway to creative flow. Imagine for a moment a beautiful, flowing stream in the woods. A large rock comes in and blocks the flow of water. Obviously, the water must re-direct and find a way around the rock, but in doing so, it loses the natural momentum and ease it had before.

The same imagery holds true when we lose our connection to self-care, compassion, and love for self. We need to be in direct connection with these three principles at all times. When we are not, we want to immediately remember where this break happened and go back into gratitude for all that we bring to this world. No accomplishment is too small to celebrate. The smaller the better when it comes to opening up the river of creativity flowing through you. Compassion for self has no guidelines, except for one: the willingness to allow yourself to feel good about yourself!

CREATING INTENTION

Intention wasn't a word I used much when I was a young dancer. In fact, I don't think it was a concept I understood until much later in life. When I use it now the awareness I bring to it is simple: to set an intention behind a goal means to understand what meaning it will bring to our lives to accomplish it. In dance we live a life of goal setting. We are always looking towards our next point of accomplishment. Sometimes I believe we may get so wrapped up in the next goal that we forget to honor the accomplishment we just obtained. It is easy to do! When we bring in the idea of setting a meaningful intention behind where we are placing our energy, we begin to open ourselves up to a deeper level of commitment to our goals. The light we shine on our deeper commitment is the best way to override the negative, critical voice inside our heads. We don't allow the critic voice to deter us, as we understand the importance and meaning behind our goals and dreams.

Sometimes the word intention may be used in place of the word goal. We may set an intention that we are aspiring to reach. In truth, they go hand in hand. A goal is the concrete tangible thing we want to experience and the intention is the energy behind the goal which keeps us focused and in beautiful alignment with the "why" behind the goal. The two cross seamlessly and are difficult to extract from one another. In essence, the intention is the energy not yet converted into form. Because intention is abstract in nature it lies here, in the heart center. Just as we bring vulnerability and artistic expression to our dancing and roles, so also do we bring intention to the goals we wish to accomplish.

EXERCISES

1. Place a hand gently on your heart center and on your belly. Take a deep breath in, connecting these two points together with an internal visual. You may add in a favorite color to connect these points or even inhale a golden healing light to fill up your chest and belly. The bigger the breath the better, relaxing and releasing any stuck energy. This will help to return your heart center and core back to a place of equal balance.

2. Before entering class today set a special intention of giving and gratitude. Give yourself permission to be creative with these concepts: using a color to replicate the energy of giving or a favorite shape or word to align with gratitude. Remembering that being given a character or part to dance is no different than using a specific visual to work with during class. Sending love to yourself while you are dancing will help you to become more open and less stuck in a rigid movement quality, which will allow that beautiful inner spark to carry through you and into your dancing!

3. Take a few moments to write down the reasons why you are working toward your goals. Ask yourself: what is the deeper meaning for me behind the choices I am making or the intended goal I am working toward? Shining a light on what accomplishing your goal will mean to you has a lovely impact on incentivizing your focus. Another approach is to also shine a light on the meaning behind the journey of accomplishing your goal. What will embarking on this new journey bring to your life?

CRITIC

A strong critic voice is the enemy of a balanced heart center. It is the little or big voice that comes in loud and clear whenever we want to take a new creative risk or try something different for ourselves. The critic voice is there to make sure we stay nice and safe and do not disrupt the very comfortable routine we have created and enjoy. It takes a great deal of courage to

> **HEART :** *Moving From Balance*
> **SOFTEN YOUR HEART**

not listen to this voice. In fact, it sometimes speaks so loudly that we don't even know we are listening to our critic; instead we believe that this superpower of negativity is how we have managed to accomplish all of our wonderful achievements so far. The critic is aligned with the mind and fear. And many use fear unknowingly, as a motivational tool to keep them focused on all the places they need improvement, so that they will work even harder to obtain their goals.

As dancers, we are always in the fear-based, result-oriented dialogue. For the most part, the dance world is set up in this framework: you are told what you need to work on, and then you fix it as quickly as possible.

Easy as that. But what if we could create a very different internal dialogue that didn't erase the critic voice entirely, but gave notice to what it was saying and then allowed space for a choice to listen or not? The act of having a choice around whether we listen or not is what gives us freedom and control of our critic voice. Without choice, we often are listening-in to a voice that is quite negative and perfectionistic in nature and responding to that voice with our beliefs about who we are and what we are allowed to dream of accomplishing.

MINDFULNESS FOR DANCERS

EXERCISES

1. Check in to see how loudly your critic voice is speaking to you. Are you using this voice as a motivator or motivational tool to push you to achieve more? Pair this inner critic with some acknowledgment and self-love for all that you have accomplished and are working toward for your best self. Remember that your critic voice, even though it may be loud, is not always accurate or true.

2. Take this critic voice into the studio with you. Write down the triggers and moments that bring out the critic voice into full force. Observe what this voice does to your movement quality, your artistic expression. Write your observations down in your journal.

3. Remember some self-care today if your critic voice seems overwhelmingly loud. Take a pause and place your hand on your heart center and breathe in - a beautiful field of flowers or a favorite color as many times as you need to remind yourself of the beauty you have inside. Remember nothing is perfect the first time around or even the second or third. Creativity and art are about being in the process and compassion for the process, not just the accomplishment and end result.

CROWN

MOVING FROM GRACE

Grace. The mere mention of that word brings a sensation of calm to my being. Grace in dance is a given. It doesn't matter the type or style of dance. To be a dancer of any kind inspires grace, as it is other worldly to be able to move the way dancers do. To be in a wondrous flow of artistry with our movements is to be in grace with our bodies. We are in a different place in which time and space flow effortlessly in sync and we move as if we are free from any earthly constraints. It is an impulse held deep within our body that instinctively tells us what to do. We are in grace with ourselves as our technique and our artistry become one.

In the energy world, the top of the head is referred to as the crown, the place within the body where one can connect to a larger, more expansive version of themselves, something "universally other." The crown of the head is the farthermost point on our body and has the capacity to hold and remember a more expansive version of our small selves. It is sometimes referred to as a special doorway to higher consciousness and creative light. It is also the place that we most often refer to as the place where our artistry originates, as it offers an elusive, abstract connection point to something indescribable. I am drawn to this energy point because it links the body into grace— the grace of a fluid stream of energy that guides us through our movements and allows an awakened sense of self that is expansive and whole. As dancers we are always graceful, but the idea of grace that I am working with here is that of witnessing yourself from a new perspective, one that sees the body as energy and the expression of that energy in its purest form. Think of grace as the highest, most pronounced expression of yourself through your movement, of grace as artistry.

In order to move from grace, we must allow ourselves to let go of all the technical chatter in our minds. This chatter only gets in the way of our artistic voice and keeps us locked in a bland replication of our technique. It is the difference between being a dancer and being an artist. The dancer produces wonderfully proficient movements, while the artist uses movement as the medium for deeper expression. Imagine your thumbprint for a moment. It is yours and yours alone. Through your dancing you are the expression of that thumbprint, the personal you, the artist.

EMBARKING ON A WISH

A wish is most often something that we want to become. It is often this beautiful representation of our best self out in the near or distant future. We witness this wish for ourselves in a bold format. A wish presents a vision of the future that is enticing. It serves as a fabulous and motivating force to help us grow into the best version of our small selves. A wish is a vision or a desire that is not always easily attainable, but something that is hoped for and sought after as a moment of positive change for our lives.

I love spending time dreaming of projects I want to pursue. I deliberately choose things that will push all of my buttons, such as starting a business or writing a book, for example. I like to have a very deep connection with the creative process of any project. Watching your own idea take shape is an incredible journey and one that is quite transformational.

As dancers, we are so lucky to have multiple opportunities to create future dreams. We get to wish for a future part to come our way or a company we would like to join. In fact, there are so many opportunities to get excited about that it can be overwhelming. It can become easy to stay rooted in the "dream phase" of life. But there must be a moment when you allow yourself to commit to embarking on the execution of your wish and take baby steps toward the full creation of that sought after wish.

One of the biggest sticking points for many dancers and non-dancers alike is the idea that the universe will provide them with their dream. They have decided that they don't need to formally set anything into action, as it may inhibit the path that will come to them in time. In some ways this is completely true, but in many ways it offers a great reason for hiding out and not putting in the effort necessary to fully go after what you want.

I can't speak for the universe, but after working with many individuals on their projects I can say that the best way to invite change is to honor the wishes that you have and admit to their existence. The sheer act of even writing them down on a piece of paper can serve as a first step. Imagine that you are sitting on a couch, just hanging out, waiting for something to come to you. And you are waiting and waiting and nothing comes. You must at least get yourself up and off the couch to witness things through a new vantage point. Once this is done things always become a bit clearer and you may just happen to see the next step you will need to take for your wish to come true.

EXERCISES

1. Ask yourself this question: what is my greatest wish for myself at this time? Be bold here and write it down. There may be more here than just one, so put them all down in your journal.

2. Another question: what are a few of the fears and personal blocks standing in the way of me obtaining my wish? Remember that shining a light on your fears may be uncomfortable, but a necessary step in bringing you closer to the completion of your wish.

3. Last question: what are my strengths and gifts that will help me to obtain this wish? Give yourself some love and encouragement here as to why this wish will be able to be accomplished. Once you have walked through these questions, you may then set three action steps to begin working toward your goal.

VISUALIZATION

I used visualization regularly during my dancing days. In fact, I used it to achieve most any of the long shot future wishes and goals to which I put my mind. When I have wanted something to become reality the

> ➤ **CROWN** : *Moving From Grace*
> **MANIFEST YOUR DREAMS**

use of daily visualization has worked tremendously well. I remember the first time I used this when I was a young dancer. I really wanted to be the Snow Queen in the Nutcracker. Unfortunately, I wasn't one of the dancers shortlisted for the part. But I was determined. I worked hard in class and then every night as I went to sleep, I put my head phones on and listened to the music. I visualized myself getting the part. And you know what? I did.

I am a firm believer in the act of bringing something hidden into the light, which is exactly what you are doing when you use this tool. We are using the play between our conscious brain and its reality-based focus and our subconscious brain and its more expansive

dreaminess. In essence, we take our hidden dreams and wishes and turn them into reality. Since our subconscious mind has no idea that something is unobtainable, it is our best tool for reprogramming our limited vision of what is possible.

Visualization works through the habit of practice. It must become a daily habit because you are literally taking the dream seed from your subconscious and overriding the conscious brain and its hold over you. As a dancer, this tool can be used to create more pirouettes, longer balances, or anything over which you want to expand your range of movement.

The tool may be practiced anytime but a particularly good time is at night, just before you go to bed. This is because you are working with the subconscious brain, which is truly aware and open at night for processing. If you visualize yourself smoothly executing your movement right before bed, you are feeding the subconscious mind visual information that will come into play when you go to do your movement. The subconscious can then override the fear and negation of the conscious brain easily, similar to the way a new groove can be created in your brain through repetition.

EXERCISES

1. Sun above your head: Sit in a quiet space either in the morning or evening and envision a large sun right above your head. This sun may be as big as you like. It may even fill the room. Sit under your personal sun and allow it to spill over and down through the top of your head, filling your entire body with golden, healing light. Allow it to penetrate and warm every cell in your being. Sit under this light until you feel energized and more like your vibrant self, alive to your connection to grace.

2. Choose the future vision you would like to see yourself achieve and begin focusing on it before bed and throughout your day. Practice with a calm mind and calm heart. See yourself as effortless in your vision: you are doing everything naturally and with ease. This practice will train the mind to release any nervousness or energy that is blocking the accomplishment of your vision for yourself.

3. If your world is spinning, you have lost your sense of trust and place within the universe. Remember you are only a small but instrumental part in this much larger, more expansive world. Find a quiet space to do a simple meditation. Take some deep breaths, filling up the lungs and releasing with the exhale any stress that is present. Sit for 5 minutes in silence, bringing the focus back to your breath and the simplicity of just giving yourself this time. Allow for silence, space, and stillness.

As I send you off on your journey through dance, I hope you have gained some valuable mindfulness tools to support you inside and outside the studio. Mindfulness is an approach to anything. It is a step back from spinning thoughts and ingrained habits to momentarily pause and embrace love. Love for all that you are and bring to your world.

Love is simple. It is choosing to find the humor in life when things have gotten too serious or choosing to find a glimmer of joy each and every day. I am reminded there is nothing more, better, or profoundly healing to all hearts, minds, and souls. And when love is pulled apart and broken down to its simplest form, then compassion, warmth and forgiveness can be embraced.

Remember, the simplest truths with the most value are often the easiest to overlook, so know that you hold the power to drop back into the mindset of love anytime you wish!

With love on your journey,
Cory

ACKNOWLEDGEMENTS

I wish to send a big hug to those who have helped and supported me with the writing, editing and final production of this book! Bringing any idea from creative seed to final form is a big journey and one that takes an amazing amount of patience and focus!

I would like to humbly acknowledge my writing coach, Deborah Siegel and Coray Ames Hoffner, my editor. They were both so kind and professional as they walked me through the ins and outs of the writing process. I have learned a great deal from each of them and feel so honored that they were supporting me at every step.

On the visual side, I have a deep appreciation for the work of Nancy Palmer, my graphic designer and Cody Pickens, my dance photographer. They are a beautiful team and have so much love for what they do. It was a joy to work with both of them.

And lastly, I have been so lovingly held by my husband, who is always there for me with any project I decide to jump into. He holds no expectations and listens patiently for hours, days, and weeks if necessary, as I walk through my creative process. My children are also the loves of my life and are always there and willing to give me lots and lots of mama hugs! My parents and sister are a continuous resource and foundation for my writing at all turns. And, my dearest friend, Melanie Henderson Batycky, who without her insight here and there, I wouldn't have been able to write this book! Thank you!

ABOUT THE AUTHOR ✑

Coach, writer, teacher, mother, intuitive, and former professional ballet dancer, **Corinne Haas** has performed with companies including Alonzo King LINES Ballet, San Francisco Ballet, and the San Francisco Opera Ballet. Passionate about inspiring others to cherish and love themselves more deeply, she has her own intuitive coaching business, Transformational Coaching for Women, where she dedicates her gifts as an intuitive healer to help guide and support lasting change among her clients. She has taught workshops based on her Artistry Workbook for pre-professional dancers in the Bay Area at Alonzo King LINES Ballet, Dominican College and Mills College. She has been published in Dance Magazine: "Visualize Success: 3 Ways To Become A Better Auditioner" to help aid young dancers with the audition process. She lives happily in San Francisco with her husband and two wonderful boys.

CREDITS ✑